CONTENTS

THE SQUARE MILE

DID YOU KNOW?

The City is full of historical 'firsts' and 'oldests', including the oldest continuously inhabited room, which is in the hall of the Vintners' Company and predates the Great Fire of London. It has the oldest continuous system of government in the UK, was the first city to elect its own Chief Magistrate and is the place where organisations, including the Samaritans and the Methodist Church, were first established.

We can thank the Romans for founding the City of London, naming it Londinium, and for its descriptive nickname of 'The Square Mile'. The initial Roman settlement, which was founded around AD 43, didn't last long and was burned to the ground by Boudicca, the warrior queen, in about AD 60.

The Romans learned the lessons of this native rebellion and erected a wall around the new trading port on the north bank of the Thames. It was approximately one Roman square mile (1,000 paces or 5,000 feet). However, this was never square – it was an irregularly shaped area that followed the line of the river as its southern boundary.

London covers 600 square miles and has a population of 8.6 million, but only its oldest part, just one square mile in size, is called the City of London. The City of London (the City) has expanded slightly over the centuries and now encompasses

The City skyline and Blackfriars Bridge at sunrise.

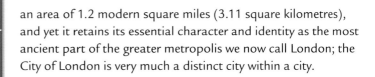

The City blends the ancient and the modern seamlessly. While the City has the greatest concentration of financial and professional services businesses in the world, it is also home to the College of Arms, which is a branch of the Royal Household responsible for granting and regulating the use of coats of arms in much of the Commonwealth.

an area of 1.2 modern square miles (3.11 square kilometres), and yet it retains its essential character and identity as the most ancient part of the greater metropolis we now call London; the City of London is very much a distinct city within a city.

The settlement achieved a population of 60,000 just 40 years after its foundation and became the largest city north of the Alps. The ravages of the plague in the early middle ages are estimated to have killed one in three of the population and plague pits have been revealed during recent excavations for the new Crossrail.

The Great Fire of London in 1666 is the most famous of the many fires that engulfed parts of the City. The fire raged for five days and is estimated to have consumed 13,200 houses, as well as St Paul's Cathedral, 87 churches, six chapels, Guildhall, the Royal Exchange, the Custom House, numerous livery company halls, three gates and four stone bridges. Sir Christopher Wren's plans for the design of a new metropolis of wide open streets wasn't to be, as land owners wanted to regain the land they owned in the City prior to the fire. As a result the City's street layout is still essentially medieval in origin.

The Second World War bombing, widely known as the Blitz, resulted in the destruction of much of the ancient City, including many of the Livery Halls and the roof of Guildhall. St Paul's was hit but survived thanks to the efforts of the Fire Watch. Other densely packed areas such as the Barbican were reduced to rubble and not fully redeveloped until the 1970s.

Deregulation of the financial markets in 1986, otherwise described as the 'Big Bang', heralded the advent of computer-based trading and the influx of American and other foreign firms into the Square Mile. It set the City on the path to becoming the world's largest financial services centre, surpassing New York.

The residential population of the City in modern times is only about 7,000, yet more than 400,000 people commute into the City during the working week. During business hours the City is a hive of commercial activity; it is the most economically prosperous and productive part of the UK, and a global hub for financial and professional services. Despite this, at the weekends and away from the tourist hot spots, the City can seem almost abandoned.

The City has its own unique system of government, its own police force and its own civil and criminal courts. It is not a borough of Greater London; rather it is a ceremonial county, the smallest in the UK, with its own elected Sheriffs and, most importantly, its Lord Mayor – who should never be confused with the Mayor of London.

The City's government is one in which residents, businesses and members of the City's guilds (known as Livery Companies) all participate in voting. The Sheriffs are elected by the Liverymen of the City's guilds and the candidates for Lord Mayor are approved by them before being elected.

The Court of Common Council predates parliament and has the power to amend its own constitution, a privilege not granted to any other city, town or other local government in the UK. It is also the only city mentioned by name in Magna Carta; a clause still in effect today confirms the City's ancient rights and privileges that already existed long before that famous document was written. In fact, the City's government is so ancient that it has no founding document or constitution; it exists by prescription.

◄ One of the original City of London dragons that marked the entrance to the City.

▲ Statue of railway engineer James Greathead on Cornhill. Greathead invented the tunnelling shield needed to dig the Tube system.

◄ The City's modern skyscrapers, including the Walkie Talkie, the Cheesegrater and the Gherkin.

It is because of the ancient and unique nature of the Square Mile, rather than in spite of it, that the City is able to blend the past with the present so successfully. In 2017 the venture capital investment in the City's technology services businesses reached a record £2.5 billion, a figure four times larger than Paris, its nearest European rival. In the same year, the City elected the 690th Lord Mayor of London in what is possibly the oldest, continuous civic ceremony in the UK.

The Square Mile has always been a place of commerce, where merchants traded, craftsmen toiled, financiers lent money and taxes were collected. In the 21st century, the City's businesses are largely focussed on financial, professional and technology-based services, including banking, insurance, investment, commodities trading, marketing, legal services, information technology, telecommunications and all the facets of the globalised information economy.

Since the 1980s the City has seen many tall buildings reach above the height of St Paul's Cathedral, which until 1967 was the tallest building in the City. Some of the more notable skyscrapers include: Tower 42 on Old Broad Street, originally called the NatWest Tower; 30 St Mary Axe, known as the Gherkin; 122 Leadenhall Street, known as the Cheesegrater; and 20 Fenchurch Street, known as the Walkie Talkie, which is home to the Sky Garden.

MANSION HOUSE

◀ The Palladian facade of Mansion House – home to the Lord Mayor of London.

The principal civic building in the Square Mile is Mansion House, home to the Lord Mayor of London for his or her one-year term of office. Mansion House was designed by George Dance the Elder and built between 1739 and 1752. The first Lord Mayor to move in was Sir Crispin Gascoigne in 1752, although work continued on Mansion House until 1758 and there have been many subsequent alterations and refurbishments. Prior to 1752, the Lord Mayor would usually set up office in the hall of his Livery Company, or sometimes his own home.

Mansion House has been described as the grandest tied cottage in England, although the Lord Mayor's apartment is relatively modest and most of the House has been given over to the cavernous banqueting hall, known as the Egyptian Hall, and other reception and meeting rooms. It houses a collection of Dutch and Flemish landscape, still life and seascape paintings donated by the widow of Baron Samuel of Wych Cross in 1987.

Mansion House is the scene of magnificent White Tie banquets throughout the year, including the annual Mansion House Speech by the Chancellor of the Exchequer, and many Livery Company civic banquets at which the Lord Mayor is a guest in his own home. When the Lord Mayor makes his entrance, it is usually announced by a trumpet fanfare.

However, it is not all fanfares and fine dining as there are also a number of jail cells to be found deep within the building. Mansion House used to be the Magistrate's Court for the City of London and, as the City's Chief Magistrate, the Lord Mayor used to dispense summary justice as any magistrate's court does today. Nowadays the Court has moved just across the road, but the Lord Mayor's role as Chief Magistrate continues and he or she sits in judgement of a summary trial at the Old Bailey on several occasions during the year.

GUILDHALL

The seat of the City's government is Guildhall, an early medieval structure with modern extensions that is located on the site of earlier civic buildings, which includes a Roman amphitheatre – parts of which are on view from within Guildhall Art Gallery. The most ancient part of Guildhall is the medieval crypt dating from 1411, although documentary records refer to an earlier Guildhall as far back as 1128. As with so much else about the City of London, Guildhall's origins are lost deep in the past, and even the oldest records speak only of a place already in everyday use and not why or when it was founded.

Guildhall complex is centred on the cavernous Great Hall, which is the second largest civic building in the UK; only Westminster Hall in the Palace of Westminster is larger. The Great Hall is where the City's government meets nine times a year and where civic banquets in honour of foreign heads of state are held. By custom, the Lord Mayor of London always entertains foreign heads of state after they have dined at Buckingham Palace. The dining capacity in Guildhall is substantially larger than Mansion House; a banquet given in honour of Sir Winston Churchill was recorded as having more than 800 seated guests.

Much of the Guildhall complex is given over to offices, meeting rooms and the Mayor's and City of London Court (the county court for the City), but it is also a significant public space, and Guildhall Yard is the scene of many annual ceremonies, a regular farmers' market and a wide array of cultural events, including an annual Beerfest in July run by the City Music Foundation. Guildhall also links with the Guildhall Art Gallery where much of the City's artwork is on display.

▼ The Great Hall, where civic banquets in honour of visiting foreign heads of state are held.

BANK OF ENGLAND

The Old Lady of Threadneedle Street is the popular name for England's reserve bank, which occupies a commanding site in the centre of the City opposite Mansion House. The Bank of England building is often confused with the nearby Royal Exchange, which is grander and more accessible. This confusion arises because the Bank is hidden behind a high surrounding fortresslike wall that obscures its interior complex of buildings and courtyards. While the main entrance is on Threadneedle Street, the overall effect is such that whichever side of the Bank you are looking at, it appears to be the back entrance.

The 'Old Lady of Threadneedle Street' is at the financial heart of the City.

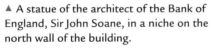

▲ A statue of the architect of the Bank of England, Sir John Soane, in a niche on the north wall of the building.

The Bank of England was founded in 1694 as England's, and later the United Kingdom's, Central Bank. Its first home was in the hall of the Worshipful Company of Mercers. The first Governor of the Bank of England was Sir John Houblon who served from 1694 to 1697. Sir John had been Master of the Grocers' Company in 1690–91, and he also served as Lord Mayor in 1695 and a Lord Commissioner for the Admiralty during his tenure as Governor.

The Bank didn't stay in the Mercers' Hall for very long, and just seven months after opening it moved to the Grocers' Hall where it stayed until 1734. It then moved to its current location on Threadneedle Street and grew over the next two centuries to occupy an entire City block. From the time of the Gordon Riots in 1780 until 1973, the Bank had a nightly military guard called the Bank of England Picquet that was provided by the Guards regiments that also stand guard outside Buckingham Palace.

In modern times, the Bank of England has autonomy in managing monetary policy for the UK economy and sets the base interest rate to manage inflation. The Bank issues the banknotes in circulation in England and Wales, a role it has performed since 1694. It also holds the national gold reserves for the UK and many other countries. A 2017 report suggested that the Bank of England's vaults held around 3 per cent of all the gold mined in the world throughout history. So significant and respected is the City's bullion market that the standard gold bar is known throughout the world as 'London Good Delivery'.

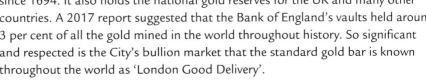

ST PAUL'S CATHEDRAL

The origins of St Paul's Cathedral stretch back to the dark ages when little written history was recorded. The first cathedral on the site was founded in AD 604 on the highest point in the City. It remained there until 675 when it burned down. Several later structures were also consumed by fire or attacks by Viking raiders, and it wasn't until 1087 that a longer-lasting cathedral was built, itself consumed in the Great Fire of London of 1666.

The architect of the cathedral we see today was Sir Christopher Wren. Wren's cathedral was begun in 1675 and finished in 1710, although some works continued up to 1720. Wren lived to see his work completed, and Wren's son

Sir Christopher Wren's masterpiece was started in 1675 and completed in 1710.

◀ St Paul's iconic dome with its famous 'whispering gallery', which makes a whisper against its walls audible on the opposite side.

and the son of the Master Stone Mason jointly laid the last stone of the building's structure. Wren is buried in St Paul's and his tomb invites those who seek his monument to 'look around you'. Several other national heroes are also buried in the crypt of St Paul's, including Vice-Admiral Horatio Nelson and the first Duke of Wellington.

The most iconic feature of St Paul's is its towering dome, which reaches to 365 feet in height. Within the dome is the famous 'whispering gallery' where the acoustics allow a hushed voice to be heard all around the interior.

Many of the City's churches were designed by Sir Christopher Wren and Nicholas Hawksmoor, although some have fabric that reaches back to the early medieval era. A particular example is the Priory Church of St Bartholomew the Great which dates from the Norman era. There are a further 46 churches in the City, an average of one church for every 200 residents. This is a remarkably large number considering the size of the City and its small residential population, yet there used to be more than double the current number of churches, with 111 existing prior to the Great Fire. Of these, 80 were destroyed and subsequently 51 were rebuilt by Wren. The bombing in the Second World War also claimed 19 churches, and some of their sites remain today as ruins, isolated towers or gardens.

St Paul's is the seat of the Bishop of London, the third highest ranking Bishop in the Anglican Church. The Bishop of London and the Sheriffs were the most senior officials in the City until the creation of the office of Mayor (today known as Lord Mayor) in 1189.

The Cathedral continues to serve a vital role at the heart of the nation, especially for funerals of national leaders and memorial services. St Paul's was also the church in which HRH The Prince of Wales married Lady Diana Spencer on 29 July 1981. During the Lord Mayor's Show, the mayoral procession stops outside St Paul's where the Lord Mayor steps down from his golden coach and receives the blessing from the Dean of St Paul's.

MONUMENT TO THE GREAT FIRE OF LONDON

The Monument to the Great Fire of London, or simply 'The Monument', is a classical column topped by a caged viewing gallery accessible by a spiral staircase of 311 steps. It was designed by Robert Hooke and Sir Christopher Wren, and erected to remember the Great Fire of London of 1666. The Monument was also intended to be an enormous scientific laboratory with space in the column for a zenith telescope, but it proved unsuited to the purpose.

Located near to the site of Thomas Farriner's bakery, where the Great Fire began on the fateful night of 2 September 1666, the Monument is 202 feet in height and stands precisely that distance from the place where Mr Farriner's bakery was located on the aptly named Pudding Lane. The reason it was built 202 feet from the location of the fire and not at the actual place it started is that it is placed over the site of St Margaret's Church, which was the first City church to succumb to the conflagration. Thomas Farriner's maidservant was one of only a handful of persons who are known to have died in the fire – this is all the more remarkable given the absence of a fire brigade and the rapidity with which the fire spread.

The Great Fire was in fact one of several major conflagrations to burn through the City, and the Court of Aldermen had previously ordered that thatched roofing be removed and cease to be used in the Square Mile as far back as 1189, followed by an outright ban in 1212. However, this ordinance was rarely adhered to, and the City has been the site of many earlier 'great fires' – including one in 1077 that burned down the original Tower of London, leading to William the Conqueror ordering that all fires be put out before households went to bed and then relit in the morning. It is from this Royal decree that we get the word 'curfew' (from the French *couvre-feu*, meaning 'to cover fire'). It's amazing to think that for many years the City had no fire stations. Even today there is just one fire station, located on Upper Thames Street.

▲ The Monument is topped by a gilded ball of flames.

◄ The Monument's height matches the distance from where the Great Fire of London started on Pudding Lane.

OLD BAILEY

The Central Criminal Court, more commonly known as the Old Bailey, has a long history of dealing with some of the most serious cases of murder, manslaughter and terrorism. The current building dates from 1907, although the Court has been on the site since 1674. The Old Bailey takes its name from the street that was on the exterior of the City's ancient defensive wall (the Bailey). An even earlier Court was adjacent to the old Newgate Prison on the site of the City's New Gate; a cell

▲ The Old Bailey's famous gold-leaf statue of Lady Justice, holding a sword in one hand and the scales of justice in the other.

◄ The Central Criminal Court of England, as it is officially known, is one of a number of buildings housing the Crown Court.

that is believed to be from this prison remains in the basement of the Viaduct Tavern opposite the modern Old Bailey complex on Newgate Street.

In times past, convicts who were sentenced to death would be kept in the cells in the Old Bailey before being carted off to Tyburn (near Marble Arch) to meet their grizzly fate. From 1783 executions were carried out on the scaffold outside the prison. To this day there is a long walkway within the complex that is still known as 'dead man's walk'. Crowds would gather outside laden with stones and rotten food to throw at the condemned.

The Old Bailey has a total of 18 courtrooms, and the centre seat in each is reserved for the use of the Lord Mayor of London, who sits in court during a ceremonial opening held several times during the year. The Lord Mayor takes precedence over all other judges in the Old Bailey, although he or she no longer routinely sits to hear criminal cases.

Unlike all other courts in the United Kingdom, the City of London Corporation rather than the Ministry of Justice runs the Old Bailey. The operational head of the Old Bailey has the grand title of Secondary and Undersheriff of London, and the most senior of the judges goes by the title of the Recorder of London.

The City's two Sheriffs stay resident in the Old Bailey during their year in office and are responsible for its ceremonial opening every day the Court sits. The Sheriffs also entertain the judges by inviting guests from across the City's civic, commercial and social institutions to dine with them at lunchtime.

CITY BRIDGES

London's iconic Tower Bridge is just outside the Square Mile, but is owned and operated by the City of London Corporation, which is also responsible for the upkeep and policing of four other bridges. Heading upstream from Tower Bridge (opened 1894), they are: the modern London Bridge (1973), Southwark Bridge (1921), the Millennium Bridge (2002) and Blackfriars Bridge (1869).

All the City's bridges are funded by the Bridge House Estates, a charitable trust that owns property throughout the Square

DID YOU KNOW?

Every year over 600 Freemen of the City of London exercise their right to herd sheep across London Bridge in an annual 'Sheep Drive' that raises money for the Lord Mayor's Appeal and other charities. The event is organised by the Worshipful Company of Woolmen and takes place on the third or fourth Sunday in September.

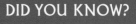

In 1952 Tower Bridge began to open as a bus was crossing, and the driver had to accelerate to jump across the opening, injuring several passengers.

◄ Although it is outside the Square Mile, Tower Bridge is owned and operated by the City of London Corporation.

Mile – including notably the Old Bailey. The surplus generated by the Bridge House Estates is sufficient to maintain all the City's bridges and the Trust disperses many millions of pounds to charitable causes each year.

London Bridge has been rebuilt several times, most recently between 1967 and 1973 when the previous bridge was sold to an American, Robert McCulloch of McCulloch Oil, and installed in Lake Havasu City, Arizona. One urban myth you may hear is that the Americans thought they were buying Tower Bridge, but there's no truth in this as the particulars of the sale were widely known at the time and handled by Ivan Luckin, an elected member of the Court of Common Council and Liveryman of the Worshipful Company of Marketors who originally proposed the sale of the bridge.

Tower Bridge is the most iconic of London's bridges, with its twin Gothic towers. It was opened in 1894 by the Prince of Wales, the future Edward VII. The bridge was built with a roadway which could be opened so that ships could pass through into the Pool of London, at a time when it was still a busy part of the river; river traffic still has precedence over road traffic. There is less river traffic now, but the bridge still opens about 1,000 times each year. A high-level footway was built to allow people to cross when the bridge was open, and it is now part of a visit to the Tower Bridge Exhibition, and offers great views over London.

◄ Looking west, from Tower Bridge to Blackfriars Bridge.

CITY MUSEUMS AND GALLERIES

DON'T MISS

Children visiting the Museum of London will especially enjoy seeing the Lord Mayor's coach and learning all about the Great Fire of London.

There is a plethora of museums and exhibits in the City. Some we have listed here, and you'll find a larger list in the Essential Information section.

Museum of London

The principal museum in the Square Mile is the Museum of London, which is open throughout the year and routinely ranked among the top museums in the UK, usually a close second to the British Museum. The Museum of London traces the history of the City from its Roman origins through to modern times. It has an immense array of exhibits, far too many to display, and runs a regular series of special exhibitions in addition to hosting many free public lectures run by Gresham College. Entry to the museum is free and ideally suited to families.

Bank of England Museum

The Bank of England has its own compact and fascinating museum that is open Monday to Friday, and on the Saturday of the Lord Mayor's Show. Entrance is free and there is an excellent small shop selling numismatic treasures and other keepsakes. The museum tells the story of the development of banking, coinage and notes in England, and the role of the Bank of England in modern times. Among the many fascinating objects on display is a gold bar made to the London Good Delivery standard that visitors can lift to experience its weight.

City Police Museum

Located within the Guildhall complex and opened from Monday to Saturday, this museum showcases the City of London Police, which is a separate constabulary from the Metropolitan Police covering the Greater London area. The City of London Police was founded in 1839, taking over the responsibilities of the day and night watches that were led by the City's two Sheriffs. In the 21st century, the City of London Police continues to deal with routine policing matters but has special responsibility for economic crime across the United Kingdom.

▼ Museum of London traces the history of the City from its Roman origins through to modern times.

Dr Johnson's House

This small City gem is tucked away at 17 Gough Square just north of Fleet Street. It is the only survivor of many London properties that were owned by Dr Samuel Johnson and the one in which he wrote the *Dictionary of the English Language*. Opening times are Monday to Saturday except in the last two weeks of December. Members of the National Trust receive a 50 per cent discount on admission.

LOOK OUT FOR DR JOHNSON'S CAT

In Gough Square, opposite Dr Johnson's House, is a bronze statue of Hodge, Johnson's favourite cat. It sits on a copy of his Dictionary, with a pair of oyster shells, a favourite treat. It was installed here in 1997.

Guildhall Art Gallery

The Guildhall Art Gallery is open daily and is home to much of the City's extensive art collection. It is also the venue for exhibitions and tours of the City's art treasures. Only about 5 per cent of the City's art collection is displayed in the gallery. The current gallery building was opened in 1999 and, during construction, the remains of the City's Roman amphitheatre were discovered. They are now on display in the basement.

▲ Guildhall Art Gallery covers works dating from 1670 to the present.

London Mithraeum

The London Mithraeum, a temple used by the Roman cult of Mithras, is located in the Bloomberg Building at 12 Walbrook. The Mithraeum was originally discovered in 1954 and relocated to Temple Court on Queen Victoria Street. After a meticulous and painstaking relocation back to the site where it was originally found, the London Mithraeum opened to the public in 2017. Entry is free but pre-booking is required. It is open from Tuesday to Sunday.

Museum of London Docklands

The Museum of London also has a branch outside the City in the Docklands area of the London Borough of Tower Hamlets. The Museum of London Docklands is open daily and explores London's trading and maritime history. The nearest stop on the Docklands Light Railway is West India Quay.

▲▲ Museum of London Docklands tells the story of the capital as a port of trade, migration and commerce.

► London Mithraeum was discovered in 1954 and opened to the public in 2017. It includes Roman objects found in recent excavations.

INNER AND MIDDLE TEMPLE

Two of London's four professional associations for barristers, collectively known as the Inns of Court, are located within the Square Mile. They are the Inner and Middle Temple, ancient institutions that reach back to the early 14th century. They are seats of learning for aspiring students of law and places of work for qualified barristers, and they also have a strong tradition of providing service to the Crown in times of crisis through the Inns of Court and City Yeomanry, a reserve forces unit closely affiliated with the Inns.

Much of the Inner and Middle Temple area is open to the public to walk around, especially the courtyards and gardens, although

▼ Although the Inner and Middle Temple buildings are private, the courtyards and gardens are usually open to the public.

◀ Temple Church was originally built by the Knights Templar in the 12th century.

the buildings are private. **Temple Church** is also worth visiting; its round shape harks back to the time when the church belonged to the Knights Templar, from which the Inner and Middle Temple derive their names. It is possible to book lunch at the Middle Temple, although there is a strict dress code and places are usually very limited. Lunch may be combined with a tour of the Temple.

The organisational structure of the Inner and Middle Temple follows that of the Oxford and Cambridge University colleges, and originally they provided accommodation in addition to office premises. They both have grand halls where students and barristers take their meals.

The UK maintains a parallel legal profession, with solicitors working directly with clients and barristers representing clients in court on both defence and prosecution sides. When a barrister is qualified they are said to be 'called to the bar', which is the dividing line between the public and the court officers. Particularly eminent barristers may be granted the title 'Queen's Counsel' or QC for short (or, when there is a king on the throne, 'King's Counsel' or KC), which confers a higher status. QCs have the right to wear a silk gown in Court, hence they are often known as 'silks'. Barristers (known as Advocates in Scotland) still wear a black gown and wig in Court in the UK and can often be seen in this formal dress in the Inner and Middle Temple.

BARBICAN CENTRE

◄ The interior of the Barbican Centre, which includes a concert hall, a theatre, an art gallery, a lending library, cinemas, restaurants, foyers and car parks.

For such a compact city, the Square Mile has many cultural destinations and experiences. Chief among these is the Barbican, a leading international arts and learning centre. The Barbican is owned and operated by the City of London Corporation, which is one of the largest sponsors of the arts in the United Kingdom.

Designed in a Brutalist style by Chamberlin, Powell and Bon, the Barbican Centre was opened by Queen Elizabeth II in 1982. The arts centre is spread over seven floors yet is well hidden within the wider Barbican Estate. It is advisable to book early for concerts and theatrical and dance performances via the Barbican's website.

The Barbican is home to the London Symphony Orchestra, and is where the Royal Shakespeare Company regularly performs. It even manages to do an impressive job of hiding the second largest conservatory in London (23,000 square feet) within its seven floors (see Parks, Gardens and Public Spaces on pages 40–41).

Located within the City's largest residential complex, called the Barbican Estate, the Barbican features several restaurants, a lakeside cafe, a concert hall, two theatres, two art galleries, exhibition halls, a shop selling art and design products, and three cinemas. The building also includes a specialist music library that runs a regular series of events and the whole complex is adjacent to the Guildhall School of Music & Drama.

▲ The Lakeside Gardens and Terrace are at the heart of the Barbican Estate. The Barbican Centre (left) is a world-class arts and learning organisation.

CULTURE MILE

The City of London Corporation, together with the Barbican, London Symphony Orchestra, Guildhall School of Music & Drama and the Museum of London are developing a major destination for culture and creativity – Culture Mile – in the north-western quadrant of the City, stretching just under a mile between Farringdon and Moorgate. Over the next decade, the area will be transformed, improving the offer to audiences with collaborations, outdoor programming, better links between venues, major enhancements to the streets and wider public realm. The aim is to enliven the area, which, as Culture Mile expands and flourishes, will be regenerated.

The City of London's ever-changing skyline. From left to right in this view are 125 Old Broad Street (Stock Exchange Tower), Tower 42 (NatWest Tower), the Cheesegrater (122 Leadenhall Street), 20 Gracechurch Street and the Walkie Talkie (20 Fenchurch Street).

THE LORD MAYOR

Even Londoners can be confused by the fact that London has a Mayor for the Greater London metropolis and a Lord Mayor for the City of London. In fact, they should be even more confused because each of London's boroughs has its own Mayor, and the City of Westminster also has a Lord Mayor, so there are in fact 32 Mayors and two Lord Mayors. All very confusing indeed, but the City of London is a special case, and the model for city and town Mayors across the UK, so we should pay particular attention to the office of the Lord Mayor of London.

Although historians differ as to when London first had a Mayor, the year 1189 has been accepted as the date from which the Mayoralty begins. The first Mayor of London was Henry Fitz-Ailwin of London Stone who served 24 years in office before wearing out his welcome. The title Lord Mayor came into use in the 14th century and later still the title expanded to become the Right Honourable the Lord Mayor of London.

The Lord Mayor takes precedence above all persons in the City, except the monarch, and is the head of the City's government and

▲ The State Coach has been used in every Lord Mayor's Show since 1757. For the rest of the year it can be seen at the Museum of London.

◄ Charles Bowman became the 690th Lord Mayor in 2017. He served as Sheriff of the City of London in 2015–16.

its Chief Magistrate. Every Lord Mayor is elected from among the Aldermen for a single one-year term. The office of Lord Mayor is unpaid; in fact, they contribute significantly from their own pockets to the cost of their year in office. While the Lord Mayor receives no salary, bonus or pension, they do get to stay in the Mansion House and travel overseas for approximately 100 days promoting the City.

The Sheriffs

The City elects two Sheriffs, of equal status, although one of them is usually also an Alderman as it is a prerequisite for progression to the office of Lord Mayor that an Alderman must have served as Sheriff in the City. Once elected, the Sheriffs receive Royal Warrants appointing them to office for a single year. The Sheriffs ran the City for many centuries prior to the office of Lord Mayor being created. They were responsible for law and order, and for tax collection. Nowadays their primary role is to support the Lord Mayor and to open the daily court sessions at the Old Bailey. The Sheriffs are provided with apartments in the Old Bailey complex so they are on hand every day the court is in session.

LIVERY COMPANIES

The City of London's Livery Companies are unique entities that grew out of the medieval craft and trade guilds that were a common feature of many European cities. Elsewhere guilds have largely died away, but in the City they have increased in number, membership and impact upon wider society through their support for a wide range of philanthropic, occupational and educational activities.

A revival in the fortunes of the City's Livery Companies began in the late Victorian era with the formation of the City and Guilds of London Institute, now the world's largest vocational examination awarding body. A hiatus of almost 200 years in the formation of new Livery Companies came to an end in 1926 when the Honourable Company of Master Mariners became the first of the 'modern' Livery Companies. The only difference between the

▲▲ The Livery Hall of the Worshipful Company of Armourers and Brasiers.

▲ The Livery Hall of the Stationers' Company was completed in 1673.

▼ The Livery Hall of the Drapers' Company, with ceiling paintings depicting Shakespearean scenes.

the Worshipful Company of Information Technologists are clearly creatures of the 20th century.

Livery Companies are still very active in their particular occupation; for example the Goldsmiths' Company run the Assay Office in London and hallmark gold, silver, platinum and palladium (precious metals); they also conduct the annual Trial of the Pyx in which the coins of the realm are tested for quality. The Gunmakers' Company test the barrels of all small-bore firearms to ensure they can withstand the pressures exerted during firing. The Fishmongers' Company still inspect the quality of fish sold at London's Billingsgate Market. Livery Companies invented the concept of the apprenticeship, and a Freeman of the City of London may still take an apprentice under his or her wing. On successful completion of the apprenticeship, the apprentice may be admitted to a Livery Company as a Freeman.

ancient and modern Livery Companies is that of age, and some very modern Livery Companies represent long-established professions such as the Worshipful Company of Hackney Carriage Drivers (for London Black Taxi drivers), a trade that has existed for centuries. Others such as the Honourable Company of Air Pilots and

Several of the Livery Companies own halls, the very grandest of which rival large stately homes and provide magnificent dining venues for the formal banquets for which they are famed. Not every Company owns a hall, and many Companies enjoy visiting other halls for their social events.

CUSTOMS AND TRADITIONS

The City of London is the setting for a truly bewildering array of ancient customs, ceremonies and traditions. The Livery Companies are responsible for maintaining many of the City's annual cycle of civic events. Each Livery Company has its own traditions, and most of the younger Companies borrow from the older Companies in their dining customs or installation ceremonies. Some of the more prominent of the various customs and traditions that are held in public include:

The Inter-Livery Pancake Races on Shrove Tuesday have become a popular lunchtime event for Liverymen, City workers and tourists. Held at midday in Guildhall Yard, the pancake races involve members of the Livery Companies running in various races while holding a frying pan and flipping a pancake. The race derives from the custom of preparing and consuming pancakes prior to the religious fast of Lent.

The United Guilds Service, held in St Paul's Cathedral during April, is a relatively recent innovation for the Livery Companies. The service was first held during the dark days of the Second World War when London was subject to sustained bombing and much of the City was in ruins. The service was an act

▶ The Shrove Tuesday Inter-Livery Pancake Race takes place in Guildhall Yard.

▼ Swan Upping on the Thames, where swans are marked to indicate ownership by the Crown.

of defiance and a morale-boosting effort. This is one of the few events when there is an opportunity to see the Lord Mayor, Sheriffs, Aldermen, Masters, Clerks and Wardens of the Livery Companies all process in their robes and insignia of office. The service is not open to the public but there is an excellent photographic opportunity to be had on the steps of St Paul's after the service as the dignitaries emerge in their finery.

The annual Cart Marking Ceremony is performed by the Worshipful Company of Carmen in Guildhall Yard on a weekday in mid-July. This ceremony involves the Master of the Carmen's Company marking each vehicle in a parade of vintage and modern wheeled conveyances as diverse as horse-drawn carriages and modern London buses.

Swan Upping is perhaps the most curious of the Livery Company traditions and takes place on the Thames during July. The Vintners' Company and the Dyers' Company share the right to mark swans with the monarch. The swans were originally taken for the dinner table by these companies, but nowadays it's an exercise in conservation and management of the population of swans on the upper reaches of the Thames.

The Boar's Head Ceremony, performed by the Worshipful Company of Butchers in December, processes from Butchers' Hall to the Mansion House whereupon the Boar's Head (now just a papier-mâché model) is presented to the Lord Mayor in payment of a fine levied upon the Company for offal thrown into the River Fleet. Usually the Boar's Head is held aloft on a large tray and carried on the shoulders of either members of the Company or one of its affiliated military units.

FREEDOM OF THE CITY OF LONDON

▲ Dame Judi Dench received the Freedom of the City of London in 2011.

► The Worshipful Company of Woolmen host an annual Sheep Drive over London Bridge.

►► Author J.K. Rowling with her Freedom of the City of London certificate at Mansion House in 2012.

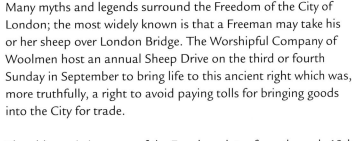

Many stars of stage, television, sport and the arts have been admitted as Freemen, including Dame Judi Dench, Sir Maurice Micklewhite (a.k.a Michael Caine), Sir Ian McKellen, Morgan Freeman, Bill Gates, Stephen Fry and many others. However, these are not, as is often described in the press and media 'honorary Freemen'; that accolade is reserved for a select few.

Many myths and legends surround the Freedom of the City of London; the most widely known is that a Freeman may take his or her sheep over London Bridge. The Worshipful Company of Woolmen host an annual Sheep Drive on the third or fourth Sunday in September to bring life to this ancient right which was, more truthfully, a right to avoid paying tolls for bringing goods into the City for trade.

The oldest existing copy of the Freedom dates from the early 13th century, although the status no doubt existed prior to that time. In times past, it was a requirement for anyone who wished to trade in the City of London to be a Freeman, and three different routes to the Freedom evolved.

They remain:

By Patrimony – a son or daughter of a Freeman born after either of their parents became a Freeman has the right to be admitted to the Freedom once they reach the age of 18.

By Servitude – an apprentice to a Freeman may be admitted as a Freeman on successful completion of his or her apprenticeship. This route is still operated by many of the Livery Companies.

By Redemption – a fit and proper person may be nominated by any two Liverymen or any two elected members of the Court of Common Council. Most admissions by Redemption are persons presented by a Livery Company.

Today the Freedom confers no particular trading rights or privileges but is a requirement for anyone wishing to stand for election in the City of London, and for progression within the Livery Companies to the status of Liveryman. Despite the term 'Freeman', women have been admitted since the earliest times.

The City of London still admits Freemen in an ancient ceremony held in Guildhall and, on rare occasions, the Freedom is conferred as an honour upon some national leader or foreign dignitary. When an Honorary Freedom is presented, the Lord Mayor, Sheriffs and Aldermen all attend, and the Freeman is invited to give a speech to mark the occasion. The Honorary Freedom has been conferred upon such eminent figures as Admiral Lord Nelson, Florence Nightingale, Sir Winston Churchill, President Nelson Mandela, Sir Tim Berners-Lee and Professor Stephen Hawking, but in all other respects, the Honorary Freedom is the same as any other Freedom of the City of London.

CITY CEREMONIAL

The City blends the ancient and the modern in a seamless manner that brings out the best of both. It throws away no tradition that it finds to be useful, and certainly the City is not short of ancient customs and ceremonies. While they are too numerous to list in detail, the following are the more prominent among them.

The Lord Mayor's Show

The highlight of the City's civic year is the annual Lord Mayor's Show, held on the second Saturday in November. The Show starts at 11 a.m. when the parade departs from Mansion House en route to the Royal Courts of Justice. It is worth turning up at least two hours in advance to see all the floats, bands and participants as they line up along London Wall, Aldersgate Street, Gresham Street and in Guildhall Yard to prepare for the start.

However, it's not just about marching bands and military personnel, as the Show includes representatives from the

DID YOU KNOW?

The Lord Mayor's Show is the BBC's longest-running annual live TV broadcast filmed outdoors. The Show was also the first public duty at which members of St John Ambulance were in attendance.

various charities supported by the Lord Mayor's Appeal, the schools affiliated with the City of London, youth groups, Livery Companies and representatives of the nations that the Lord Mayor will visit during his or her year in office.

The Show is the start of the Lord Mayor's year in office and completes a legal requirement that dates from 1215 when the City won the right to elect its own Chief Magistrate in a charter granted by King John. One of the provisions of that charter is that the City's chosen candidate 'shows' himself to the King or his justices. Today the Lord Mayor processes from Mansion House to the Royal Courts of Justice to make their declaration, stopping at St Paul's Cathedral en route to be blessed by the Dean.

The centrepiece of the Show is the Lord Mayor's gold state coach that dates from 1757. The coach is pulled by six horses; only the monarch is entitled to a greater number of horses to pull his or her state coach. The Lord Mayor's coach remains essentially unchanged since it was built, the only concession to modernity being a small light inside the cab. Rumour has it that a bunch of carrots travel with the Lord Mayor to treat the horses when the procession pauses at the Royal Courts of Justice.

◀ The State Coach is one of the highlights of the Lord Mayor's Show – a three-mile ceremony of spectacle and pageantry.

MILITARY DISPLAY

The Lord Mayor's Show is the world's largest and longest-running unrehearsed street pageant and includes more soldiers, sailors and airmen than the parade at the Sovereign's Birthday in June, otherwise known as Trooping the Colour. With the military contingent, the Show typically involves 150 separate participating organisations stretching over three miles from end to end.

The Silent Ceremony

The installation of the Lord Mayor Elect is held in Guildhall on the Friday preceding the second Saturday in November, which is the day before the Lord Mayor's Show. As the name of the ceremony suggests, it is conducted in near total silence. The only person who speaks is the Lord Mayor Elect, who makes his or her declaration of office. All the high officers of the City are present, including the Sheriffs, Aldermen, Town Clerk, Chamberlain, Swordbearer, the Common Cryer and Sergeant at Arms, among many others all in their full ceremonial dress. The ceremony is a free public event, although tickets must be obtained in advance from the City of London Corporation website and are issued by ballot.

Following the ceremony, the newly installed Lord Mayor departs for Mansion House in a Rolls Royce, but before that, the outgoing Lord Mayor asks the Swordbearer to hand over the keys to the safe in which the City of London's seal is kept. The Swordbearer removes his hat and reaches inside to extract the key from

▼ The Lord Mayor Elect is the only person who speaks at the Silent Ceremony.

▲ The Lord Mayor's Crystal Sceptre was a gift from King Henry V to the City for its support during his campaigns in France.

a pocket on the underside of the hat. He hands it to the outgoing Lord Mayor, who passes it to his successor. The newly installed Lord Mayor then returns the key to the Swordbearer and asks him to keep it safe. The Swordbearer replies, 'My Lord Mayor, I shall keep it under my hat.' This is just one of the everyday English expressions that derive from customs in the City of London.

Entry of the Monarch into the City

Whenever the monarch enters the Square Mile, the Lord Mayor greets him or her and presents the City's pearl sword as a token of feudal fealty. The monarch touches the hilt of the sword and it is returned to the Lord Mayor, thereby signifying the monarch's approval of the Lord Mayor's continued governance of the City. This ceremony is sometimes performed at the former site of Temple Bar on Fleet Street, near to the Royal Courts of Justice, but more often at the steps of St Paul's Cathedral.

▼ The Queen and the Lord Mayor of London at the service for the Order of the British Empire in St Paul's Cathedral.

Some sources have described this ceremony as one in which the monarch asks permission of the Lord Mayor to enter the City. It is a nice story, but there is no truth to it; the King or Queen of England may enter the City as they please.

PARKS, GARDENS AND PUBLIC SPACES

DID YOU KNOW?

Among the more unusual responsibilities of the City of London Corporation is that of maintaining Queen Elizabeth's medieval hunting lodge in Epping Forest.

For a city within a city, the Square Mile is blessed with an immense array of small parks, gardens and other oases of green tranquillity totalling over 150 individual spaces. **St Paul's Churchyard** is particularly popular for lunchtime picnics by City workers, as is **Finsbury Circus**, which is home to a lawn bowls club. **Postman's Park** on King Edward Street is home to the Memorial to Heroic Self Sacrifice set up by the artist and sculptor George Frederic Watts in 1900. The memorial consists of over 50 plaques that commemorate people who lost their lives saving others.

▶ The Barbican Centre Conservatory.

▼ The Sky Garden at 20 Fenchurch Street.

If the City of London's lands that lie outside of the Square Mile are included, then the City of London Corporation's estate is almost entirely forest, heath and parkland, since it owns and manages Ashtead Common in Surrey, Epping Forest in Essex, Burnham Beeches and Stoke Common in Buckinghamshire, Hampstead Heath straddling the London boroughs of Barnet and Camden, and several other large parklands and commons within the Greater London area. In total, the area of parkland, gardens, heath, woodland and pasture owned and managed by the City of London is 10,378 acres, approximately 16 times larger than the area of the Square Mile.

Barbican Centre Conservatory

The conservatory on top of the Barbican Centre is open on some Sundays and bank holidays between midday and 5 p.m. (last entry 4.30 p.m.), and during the summer months it is possible to book ahead for lunch and a guided tour; it's very popular, so book early. The conservatory is home to over 2,000 species of plants and includes ponds of tropical fish.

The Sky Garden

The Sky Garden in the glass roof space of 20 Fenchurch Street, otherwise known as the Walkie Talkie, is open to the public and features both an indoor garden and an open-air terrace. The Sky Garden is free to visit but tickets must be booked in advance.

Roman Wall

Around the year 200 the Romans built a protective wall around Londinium, stretching two miles from Tower Hill to Blackfriars, and many parts of it are still visible. A section in **St Alphage Garden**, off Wood Street, was originally part of a fort, which later became part of the wall. The red and black bricks are evidence that the wall was extensively repaired in the medieval period.

ESSENTIAL INFORMATION

The City Information Centre

Based in a single-storey building on the south side of St Paul's Cathedral, the City Information Centre is the visitor centre for the Square Mile. This is the place to go for maps, opening times, tickets, details of events, tours, talks, concerts and much more besides. The team at the Information Centre are experts on the Square Mile and also sell bus, train and tube travel cards, as well as offering Foreign Exchange services.

St Paul's Churchyard

EC4M 8BX
Opening hours: Monday to Saturday 9.30am–5.30pm, Sunday 10am–4pm.
Website: www.visitthecity.co.uk
Nearest Tube: St Paul's on the Central Line

Bank of England

Threadneedle Street, EC2R 8AH
Opening hours: The Bank is not open to the public. See Bank of England Museum for visitor access.
Website: www.bankofengland.co.uk
Nearest Tube: Bank on the Northern, Central, Waterloo & City Lines and Docklands Light Railway

Bank of England Museum

Bartholomew Lane, EC2R 8AH
Opening hours: Monday to Friday 9am–5pm and on the day of the Lord Mayor's Show.
Website: www.bankofengland.co.uk
Nearest Tube: Bank on the Northern, Central, Waterloo & City Lines

Barbican Centre

Silk Street, EC2Y 8DS
Opening hours: Monday to Saturday 10am–8pm, Sunday 11am–8pm.
Website: www.barbican.org.uk
Nearest Tube: Moorgate on the Metropolitan, Northern, Hammersmith & City Lines

The Central Criminal Court

Old Bailey, EC4M 7EH
Opening hours: Monday to Friday 10am–5pm. The Court Buildings are not open to the public, other than for public access to the Court rooms while trials are in progress.
Nearest Tube: St Paul's on the Central Line

City of London Guide Lecturers Association

The association of the official City of London Guides, trained and accredited by the City of London Corporation. Various scheduled tours are held in the City; see the Association's website for details.
Website: www.cityoflondonguides.com

City of London Police Museum (inside the Guildhall Library)

Aldermanbury, EC2V 7HH
Opening hours: Monday to Friday 9.30am–5.30pm (extended to 7.30pm on Wednesdays) and alternate Saturdays 10am–4pm (check website for details).
Website: www.cityoflondon.police.uk/about-us/ history/museum/Pages/default.aspx
Nearest Tube: Moorgate on the Metropolitan, Northern, Hammersmith & City Lines

HM College of Arms

Queen Victoria Street, EC4V 4BT
Opening hours: Monday to Friday 10am–4pm.
Website: www.college-of-arms.gov.uk
Nearest Tube: Blackfriars on the Circle and District Lines

Culture Mile

Website: www.culturemile.london
Nearest Tube: Farringdon, Barbican or Moorgate on the Metropolitan, Northern, Hammersmith & City Lines

Dr Johnson's House

17 Gough Square, London EC4A 3DE
Opening hours: Monday to Friday 11am–5pm (closed on Sundays).
Website: www.drjohnsonshouse.org
Nearest Tube: Blackfriars on the Circle and District Lines

Friends of City Churches

For opening times, events, tours and access to the City's many churches, visit the Friends of City Churches website.
Website: www.london-city-churches.org.uk

Guildhall

Gresham Street, EC2V 7HH
Opening hours: Monday to Friday 9am–5pm. Access may be restricted during sessions of Common Council or during other civic and ceremonial events.
Website: www.cityoflondon.gov.uk
Nearest Tube: Moorgate on the Metropolitan, Northern, Hammersmith & City Lines

Guildhall Art Gallery
Guildhall Yard, EC2V 5AE
Opening hours: Monday to Saturday 10am–5pm, Sunday 12pm–4pm.
Website: www.cityoflondon.gov.uk
Nearest Tube: Moorgate on the Metropolitan, Northern, Hammersmith & City Lines

Inner and Middle Temple
Middle Temple Lane, EC4Y 7HL
The grounds of the Inner and Middle Temple are open to the public but are private property and may be closed from time to time.
Nearest Tube: Temple on the Circle and District Lines

London Mithraeum
Walbrook, EC4N 8AA
Opening hours: Tuesday to Saturday 10am–6pm, Sundays/Bank holidays 12pm–5pm. Free tickets must be obtained in advance as access times are limited.
Website: www.londonmithraeum.com
Nearest Tube: Bank on the Northern, Central, Waterloo & City Lines and Docklands Light Railway

Lord Mayor's Show
Held on the second Saturday in November, starting at 11am.
Website: www.lordmayorsshow.london
Nearest Tube: Bank on the Northern, Central, Waterloo & City Lines and Docklands Light Railway

Mansion House
Walbrook, EC4N 8BH
Opening hours: Group tours can be arranged in advance.
Website: www.cityoflondon.gov.uk
Nearest Tube: Bank on the Northern, Central, Waterloo & City Lines and Docklands Light Railway

The Monument
Fish Street Hill, EC3R 8AH
Opening hours: Monday to Sunday 9.30am–5.30pm (April to September), 9.30am–5pm (October to March). Closed on Christmas Eve, Christmas Day and Boxing Day.
Website: www.themonument.org.uk
Nearest Tube: Monument on the Circle and District Lines

Museum of London
London Wall, EC2Y 5HN
(Note: Museum of London is scheduled to relocate to West Smithfield in the former General Market Building in 2022.)
Opening hours: Monday to Sunday 10am–6pm.
Website: www.museumoflondon.org.uk
Nearest Tube: Barbican on the Circle, Hammersmith & City, Metropolitan Lines

Open House London (weekend)
On the third weekend in September some of the private buildings in the City open their doors to the public, including several of the Livery Halls. Entry is by tickets, which must be obtained in advance.
Website: www.openhouselondon.org.uk

Silent Ceremony (Guildhall)
Guildhall, EC2V 5AE
Held on the Friday immediately prior to the Lord Mayor's Show. Free tickets must be obtained in advance from Guildhall. Tickets are limited and are allocated by ballot.
Website: www.cityoflondon.gov.uk
Nearest Tube: Moorgate on the Metropolitan, Northern, Hammersmith & City Lines

The Sky Garden
20 Fenchurch Street, EC3M 8AF
Free tickets must be obtained in advance as access times are limited.
Website: skygarden.london/sky-garden
Nearest Tube: Monument on the Circle and District Lines

St Paul's Cathedral
St Paul's Churchyard, EC4M 8AD
Opening hours: Monday to Saturday 8.30–4.30pm.
Website: www.stpauls.co.uk
Nearest Tube: St Paul's on the Central Line

Tower Bridge
Tower Bridge Road, SE1 2UP
Opening hours: Monday to Sunday 10am–5.30pm (April to September), 9.30am–5pm (October to March). Closed on Christmas Eve, Christmas Day and Boxing Day.
Website: www.towerbridge.org.uk
Nearest Tube: Tower Hill on the Circle and District Lines

GLOSSARY

Alderman – an elected officer in the City of London's upper chamber. One Alderman is elected for each of the 25 Wards.

Apprentice – a young person (school leaver) undergoing a period of occupational training, while in employment, under the supervision of a Freeman of the City of London. Apprenticeships involve a combination of formal education, occupational training, work placement and mentorship.

Chamberlain – a senior salaried officer of the City of London Corporation who performs the role of chief finance officer.

Coat of Arms – an arrangement of divisions and symbols (known as charges) on a shield, surmounted by a helm and crest, which is granted by Letters Patent to a single person and their heirs or to a body corporate.

Common Council – the chamber of 100 elected members of the City of London Corporation.

Common Councilman – an elected officer in the City of London's lower chamber. Two or more Councilmen are elected for each Ward.

Common Hall – an assembly of the Liverymen of the several Livery Companies called for the purpose of electing the Lord Mayor, Sheriffs and certain other officers.

Freedom – the status of being admitted into a Livery Company or the City of London, historically an important rite of passage for those who wished to trade in the City. Still required for elected office and progression to Liveryman.

Freeman (of the City) – a person who has been admitted into the Freedom of a City after making a declaration. There are three routes to becoming a Freeman: by Patrimony, Redemption and Servitude.

Freeman (of a Company) – a person who has been admitted into a Livery Company.

Livery – a collective noun for the senior members of the Livery Companies and sometimes used to refer to the Livery Companies; also the robes worn by Liverymen of those Companies.

Liveryman – a senior member of a Livery Company, entitled to participate in elections of the Sheriffs and Lord Mayor.

Livery Company – an occupational Guild in the City of London. One whose senior members participate in the election of the Lord Mayor, Sheriffs and certain other ancient officers. Livery Companies are ranked in a strict order of precedence and are active in philanthropy, education, fellowship and support to their respective trade, craft or profession. They maintain close bonds with the Armed Forces of the Crown and the Church of England.

Master – the officer of a Livery Company Court and the senior Liveryman of the Company. Elected from among the members of the Company's Court, usually for a one-year term. May also be titled Prime Warden or Upper Bailiff.

Patrimony – the system by which a Freeman's children may become Freemen of the City of London if either of their parents were Freemen before they were born.

Redemption – the system by which admission to a Livery Company is obtained on payment of a fine and fulfilment of the Company's other membership criteria.

Servitude – the system by which an apprentice may become a Freeman of the City of London on completion of a period of apprenticeship under the supervision of a Freeman.

Sheriff – an elected officer in the City of London exercising royal authority; first recorded in the 7th century. Nominally responsible for protecting Her Majesty's judges.

Ward – an electoral sub-division of the City, headed by an Alderman. Two or more Common Councilmen are elected by the residents and businesses in each of the 25 Wards.